21

Teen Devotionals...
for Guys!

Paul Hart and CJ Hitz

Find Your
True Strength
.com

Published by FindYourTrueStrength.com
ISBN: 978-1493650392

Get More Information At:
www.FindYourTrueStrength.com

CONTENTS

INTRODUCTION

We live in a world that idolizes strength. We're told early on in life that real men suck it up, toughen up, and are the strong ones. But the Bible tells us to live, not as the world teaches, but to be set apart. Romans 12:2 says it this way: *"And do not be conformed to this world, but be transformed by the renewing of your mind, that you may prove what is that good and acceptable and perfect will of God."*

As Christians, we need to allow ourselves to be transformed by God – drawing from His strength (Ps. 28:7). So throughout this book, you'll find 21 devotions written with today's teen guys in mind. We hope that they will help you find your true strength in Christ.

In the 21 devotions that follow, you'll find lessons God has taught us, usually using something from our own lives to open our eyes. Each devotion is followed by a reflection question, application step, and prayer starter so that you can apply what we've learned to your own life and hopefully grow stronger in your walk with Christ.

Jesus answered, "It is written: 'Man does not live on bread alone, but on every word that comes from the mouth of God.'"
- Matthew 4:4 NIV

REAL MEN

Written by CJ Hitz

"Truthful words stand the test of time, but lies are soon exposed."
- Proverbs 12:19 NLT

Anyone can go with the flow but it takes a real man to go against popular opinion and take a stand for Truth.

In a July 2007 issue of *Blender* magazine, a Trojan condom ad appeared within its pages. The ad shows a bunch of pigs in a bar sitting, drinking and conversing with visibly annoyed women. Standing at the bar is a smiling guy and girl. The tag line reads, "Evolve. Be a man. Use a condom every time. Nobody likes a pig."

Wow, how pathetic.

We live in a culture that sets such a low standard of what it means to be a "real man." It's a culture of mediocrity and compromise at every turn. It's a culture that encourages us men to turn our backs on God and the truth of His Word regarding issues of purity.

I'm so thankful our Father in heaven has given us a different standard to live by. It's a standard that goes beyond just a physical act and into the realm of our hearts...

"A good person produces good things from the treasury of a good heart, and an evil person produces evil things from the treasury of an evil heart. What you say flows from what is in your heart."
– Luke 6:45 NLT

Apart from God, we're unable to attain a "good heart" that Jesus speaks of in the verse above. By submitting our lives to Jesus, we take the first step to becoming a Real man. Let's look at a couple characteristics of what a Real man looks like...

1.) A Real man treats other guys with respect – Don't we all want this? How many of us enjoy being "dissed" by our fellow men? Webster's defines respect as "an act of giving particular attention; high or special regard."

2.) A Real man treats girls with respect – Want to see your respect for girls increase? Begin to look at them as someone's...
- Daughter
- Granddaughter
- Future wife
- Future mom

I can guarantee that if you begin to see girls through that lens above, your respect level will go through the roof! When I was in high school, I had no idea that my future wife was living on the other side of the country. We would eventually meet in college. How about you? Where is your future wife living? How is she being treated? How are you treating the future wives of guys who may be living across the country?

Luke 6:31 is known as the "Golden Rule" that Jesus gives us…

"Do to others as you would have them do to you." (NIV)

What if we tweaked that verse to say, *"Treat another man's future wife as you would have them treat yours."*

That's what I call a Real Man!

Reflection:

What are some ways you see guys disrespecting other guys? What are some common ways guys disrespect girls? What are some other examples you see in our culture of low standards and mediocrity?

Application Step:

Try going out of your way this week to see the girls you know as someone's daughter, granddaughter, future wife and future mom.

Prayer:

Lord, I'm sorry for the ways I've lived according to the low standards in our culture. Help me to be a man who stands for Truth and sets an example to those around me. Help me to truly respect my fellow man and the girls who are in my sphere of influence. Thank you for giving us such a high standard to live by… In Jesus' name, Amen.

IDOLS

Written by Paul Hart

"You shall have no other gods before Me."

- Exodus 20:13

I Just Can't Live Without It...

I wanted to ask you a question... Just simple and straight forward, answer with the first thing that pops into your head.

What's the one thing you can't live without? Is there a sport that defines you, or maybe a type of cologne? It might be your iPhone or even a skateboard. Whatever it is, we all have something. So what's your one thing?

I'll go ahead and go first. Mine is internet access. I don't know what I would do if I lost that. I don't know how I could live without it. So what about you? What's your one thing?

Got it?

Okay, now let me tell you, if you answered that question with anything other than Jesus Christ our Lord and Savior, that one thing is an idol in your life. Most of us have them, but God hates them.

He says that He is a jealous God (Ex. 20:5). He wants to come first in our lives. Before our money, before our girls, before everything.

Let me tell you something else. That iPhone isn't going to get you into heaven. No amount of money will buy your way in. It's hard to grasp that, but only having Jesus Christ as our Savior will open the pearly gates to us. If you were to die tomorrow, would any of the things that you want so badly now, mean anything then – would they seem so important?

Reflection:

What are the idols in your life? Is there more than one?

Application Step:

Confess your idols to God and ask Him to help you, not only put Him first in your life, but also to see everything else as it really is and how it relates to Him.

Prayer:

Lord God, I admit to putting earthly things above You in my life. I have idols, I know it. Help me to surrender them to You and put You first. Help me to see You as the Lord of my life, not just confess it on Sundays...

GAME DAY

Written by CJ Hitz

"But be doers of the word, and not hearers only, deceiving yourselves."

- James 1:22

Are You Ready To Suit Up?

My high school basketball coach was as intense as an Army drill sergeant. Anyone who knew Kevin McDaniel would compare him to the legendary Bobby Knight, the former men's basketball coach of the Indiana Hoosiers. "Coach McD", as we called him, would even admit that Knight had a strong influence on his fiery coaching style. I remember practices where Coach McD would have us run a drill or specific play 20+ times in a row until he saw the level of execution he desired in a real game. Though we would sometimes grumble over his perfectionist tendencies, our whining would turn to gratitude as we savored victory. We were like a well-oiled machine as each player knew his role within the framework of the team. Win or lose, we never doubted the fact that our coach did his job to prepare us for game day.

Shouldn't our experience on God's team, the Church, be similar? We read in Hebrews 5:14 (NAS) that "...solid food is for the mature, who because of practice have their senses trained to discern good and evil..." Those words "practice" and "trained" imply preparation for game day.

And when is it game day in the spiritual life? That's right, EVERYDAY!

Our enemy and his team never take a day off, always trying to set us up for defeat. When we know the Word of God and the God of that Word intimately we become a major threat to the opposition. We become sharp and sensitive to hearing God's voice and game plan for each new day. Unfortunately the Church is being trained more by the voices in our media choices than by the voice of God. We've become more familiar with Thursday evening's TV show lineup or the playlists on our iPods than we are with the words of the Author of Life. We have our hearts tuned more to the wisdom of the world than the supernatural wisdom that our Creator is waiting to pour out to us (James 1:5).

What would happen if the Church across this country of ours decided to turn off the TV for a month in order to intentionally fill that time (5 hrs/day on avg.) with a sincere seeking of the Lord? One month out of twelve or merely 8% of our total TV time. Is there a chance we would hear something from our Coach that could totally change the momentum of this spiritual war we find ourselves in? And even if we did hear that divine directive, would we put it into practice? Would we obey?

The clock is ticking. The pressure is on. You and I are well equipped.

With God alone, victory is in our grasp!

Reflection:

Are you like a well-trained athlete in practicing what you read in the Bible? How sensitive to the Lord are you in regard to making necessary changes in your media choices (TV, music, internet etc.)?

Application Step:

Find a quiet place where you can spend time reading God's Word and listening to what He wants to say. How can you put into practice what you read?

Prayer:

Lord, I want to be someone You can count on to come through on game day (everyday). Please give me a new sensitivity and discernment so I don't miss out on "key plays" and assignments You want to give me. Thank You for choosing me to be on Your team… In Jesus' name I pray, amen.

STAND STRONG

Written by Paul Hart

"Watch, stand fast in the faith, be brave, be strong."
- 1 Corinthians 16:13

Face It

I love video games. I play them on a daily basis. It's sad, but true. After a long day, playing a video game helps me unwind. When I'm mad – I play video games. They help me disconnect from my problems.

Do you have something like that?

You may or may not be into video games like me, but maybe you read books, or watch movies. Maybe you go for a run or turn up your music. Whatever it is you do to unwind, we all have something.

The problem comes, when we start using that as a way to escape reality. When it gets to the point that we use it to avoid dealing with problems. When you turn the music up so you don't have to listen to your mom or when you tune out of a conversation you don't want to be having by focusing on a game.

God wants us to face life head on. He wants us to bring our problems to Him – not drown them in alcohol or dull them with drugs. He wants us to be strong enough to face what comes our way. To stand strong and live for Him – not hide behind our ear buds or even a blade.

Reflection:

Are you letting something you enjoy become something you hide behind?

Application Step:

This week, when you are tempted to turn to your normal escape (music, games, etc.) stop and pray for God to help you face your problems and make the right decisions – ask Him if you are running away from something that you should be facing.

Prayer:

Father God, help me to face life head on. Don't let me be tempted to escape, but instead strengthen me to man up under the pressure. To stand strong for You…

WINGMAN

Written by Paul Hart

"You shall love the Lord your God with all your heart, with all your soul, and with all your strength."

- Deuteronomy 6:5

Who's Got Your Back?

Loving someone with all our strength might sound a little girly, but have you ever just had one of those friends that you would always be there for? The one that you'd back in a fight no matter how outnumbered you were? The one that you'd go everywhere with and tell everything to? You might even have more than one. They are those friends that, while we would usually use a different word, you really do love.

Have you ever thought about God like that?

The best part about having God as a friend, is that He calls it like He sees it. You might not hear Him audibly, but if you stop and listen - really listen - you'll hear His voice within you. You can't just listen to what you want to hear, you have to really listen to what He has to say. He won't just go along quietly with any harebrained scheme you come up with – but He'll tell you the difference between right and wrong and then stick by your side no matter which one you choose.

How can we say this?

A true friend (picture that in your head now) is always there for you. He's there when times are tough. He's there before a battle and he's there after it's done. He's there no matter what. And that's how God is. When we really have a relationship with Him, when we allow Him to step up and be our wingman, He will never let us down (Deut. 31:6). He speaks to us through His Word, and it sticks with us and helps us when we need it. He's always willing to listen when we reach out in prayer.

The Bible says that we're supposed to love God with all our strength. That means making Him our wingman, not just another guy we know and sometimes hang with. Now this is really tough, because we don't see Him watching our back – but that doesn't mean He's not there. When we become Christians, God sends the Holy Spirit to live inside us and promises to always look out for our best interests (Romans 8:28). We have to trust Him to live up to that promise.

Even if you don't currently consider God your wingman, He's always been willing to step up for the role – He's got your back. He always has and always will – even if you don't realize it.

But God isn't just willing to be our wingman, He's asked us to be His in return. He'd love for you to be a loyal friend to Him. To seek His opinion first and be willing to back Him in a fight. True friendship goes both ways.

Reflection:

Romans 8:28 says that God works all things together for the good of those who love Him – do you believe that? Honestly?

Application Step:

Write Romans 8:28 on a notecard and put them in your wallet, back pocket, locker – somewhere where you will see them multiple times each day.

Prayer:

Lord, I'd like You to be my wingman. To keep me accountable. To be able to know that I can always count on You. Thanks for Your willingness to be there for me…

WHAT A LOSER

Written by Paul Hart

"He who does not love does not know God, for God is love."
- 1 John 4:8

You Don't Have To Have A Girl To Be Happy.

This is one thing I have had so many problems dealing with my whole life. I was so angry, because I thought my family hated me and I was such a loser that no one at school could possibly think much of me. I was every girl's "friend," and was so easy to talk to. Yet all I wanted was for a girl to actually care about me - not just keep me in "The Friend Zone."

I tell you this not to prove what a sap I was, but to let you know that I was so busy trying to prove something to myself in this world, that I couldn't see all the amazing things that God was offering me. I know how easy it is to beat yourself up when it feels like everyone else is anyway. But when you stop to think about it, are they really beating you down, or are you doing it all by yourself?

I know how it works to wake up and not even be able to stand looking at yourself in the mirror. "What a waste of flesh," I use to say. I couldn't stand having my picture taken, because I thought I was the ugliest thing on the planet. Why else would no girl even give me a chance?

Satan's goal is to make you hate "you." He doesn't have to get anyone else to, because nobody can do a better job of it than yourself. As long as you can't stand anything about yourself, then you are absent of love.

God is Love. Where there is God, there is Love. If you can't find love for yourself and those around you then you are literally keeping God away from you. You, and only you, can change this. But if you can't see anything past how sorry a person you are, then you won't reach out for the love God has for you - and you'll end up trying to fill the void in your life any way you can.

There can be no loneliness in your life if you allow the love of God into your life.

Having friends doesn't make you cool, but to deny those who could be real friends because they don't fit what you want is going to lead you to a lonely life. That is a life I don't wish on anyone. I can't tell you enough how wonderful God's plan for you really is. When you stop trying to do it your way, and pay more attention to God's Way it is amazing how that void in your life gets smaller and smaller.

Sadly, we will never be able to do it 100% God's way. So there will always be that part of you that wants to do it yourself. The part of that that always makes me smile is knowing that God forgives if you truly feel sorry for what you do, and there is a way out of the empty feeling every time. How can anyone be lonely knowing that?

Reflection:

Are you seeing yourself as a loser, or as someone who has not looked around enough to see how awesome God's plan for your life really is?

Application Step:

The next time you start losing confidence in yourself or putting yourself down, remember that God is love – and He loves you just the way you are. Let Him fill the void for love within you.

Prayer:

Father God, thank You for loving me. Help me to remember Your love and not to beat myself up...

THE LURE OF PORN

Written by CJ Hitz

"How can a young man cleanse his way? By taking heed according to Your word."

- Psalm 119:9

Are You Playing With Fire?

Though it's been over 30 years since that day, I remember it well. I was 8 years old the first time these eyes saw pornographic images and "Pandora's Box" would be opened. Two neighborhood boys came over to my house to play like so many other days before. Whispering, one of the boys pulled a *Hustler* magazine from inside his jacket and said, "Look what we found in my dad's closet."

I was immediately drawn to the cover image of a beautiful, yet seductive-looking woman. The three of us decided to hide behind a fence nearby where we wouldn't be seen and proceeded to inspect the contents of the magazine. As each page was turned, my young, innocent eyes opened as wide as saucers with what I was seeing. Images of nude, sexually explicit images were being seared into my brain. Deep down, I knew my parents wouldn't approve of what we were looking at but, at the same time, I hadn't received the "beware of porn magazines" talk yet.

I remember how paranoid we felt about being caught while sitting there behind that fence in another neighbor's yard. Upon finishing, we decided to bury that magazine right there where we sat. I can't recall whether I went back and tried digging it up, but I do recall looking at girls and women differently from that day on. The enemy hooked an unsuspecting victim that day just as he does with countless others in their youth.

Through the years, there would be numerous other exposures to porn. In my middle school years, I would stay the night with a friend whose dad had a *Playboy* subscription. Not only would we smuggle these issues into my friend's bedroom, but when everyone (including my friend) was asleep, I'd sneak out and try to find the "stash" of older issues. Looking at these issues only gave me a deeper, unhealthy craving to look at girls with lust in my eyes. From middle school forward I was always trying to "sneak a peek" at the cleavage of girls.

During my freshman year in college, one of my friends would rent pornographic films on his way back to the dorm after work. Before long there were 10-15 lust-filled guys huddled around a TV, filling our minds with more filth. This was on the campus of a Christian university, many of us having grown up in church. I always felt so guilty afterward and I know many of the other guys did as well.

The next year, my sophomore year in college, I made a decision to commit my life to Christ and walk with him daily. For the first time in my life, I actually wanted to read my Bible. I looked forward to attending the chapels that I had dreaded only a year earlier. I was spiritually hungry and enjoyed being fed by God's word.

But I still had a lust problem. The images were still in my mind.

Though I wasn't going out looking for porn, I still had a problem with lust and masturbation. I always felt so much shame and guilt afterward. Satan was always there ready to heap on more shame.

Fast-forward to January 10th, 1998. This is the day I stumbled upon internet porn for the first time. I was new to using the internet since my family didn't have a computer. While staying with my wife's family 7 months before we were to be married, I was on their computer while they were out of town. Unexpectedly, a pop-up came onto the computer screen advertising for a casino in Vegas. It had three very scantily-clad women with a tagline that read, "Wouldn't you like to see what else is in Vegas?" Immediately, I had a thought that was no doubt planted by the enemy. That thought was, "Wouldn't you like to know what else is on the internet?"

It was as if a whole new world was opened up that day. This would begin a cycle of stumbling off and on for the next 5 years. That means I struggled 4 ½ years into my marriage. The internet made porn a much more secretive habit than ever before in history. It was a dirty little secret I was able to hide conveniently.

I've met many young men who believe their porn and lust problem will go away once they're married. I've even met guys who try to justify looking at porn as a "healthy" way of dealing with sexual energy. Nothing could be further from the truth as my own life demonstrates. My desire for porn didn't magically go away on August 15, 1998 – my wedding day. As I would secretly look at internet porn, my desire for my wife would diminish. I developed a distorted view of sex and women that lingered in my mind for years. It was a vicious cycle of viewing porn, masturbating, feeling immense shame, doing well for a while and then falling prey all over again. The more images I loaded into the "hard drive" of my brain, the more ammunition Satan and his demons had to work with and use against me.

Eventually, I had to face my dirty little secret and come clean with my wife. I also needed to have some accountability with other men as well as adding safeguards to our computer. These things can certainly go a long way in helping a person remain pure but the most important thing a person can have is a healthy fear of the Lord. God has to be our biggest Accountability Partner. Do we really want to please Him? Do we really want to obey Him? Do we believe He has our best interest in mind when it comes to sex? After all, He did create it to be good. True freedom comes when we're satisfied with God alone. When we choose to fill our minds with the Truth of God's word, we are better equipped to respond to the lies of Satan.

Shelley & I are still a work in progress but the Lord is continuing to bring healing and freedom in the area of sex. He's slowly restoring what the "locusts had eaten" in years past. I'm so thankful for a God who gives us more chances than we deserve. His mercies are new every morning!

Reflection:

Is porn something you struggle with? Can you recall the first time you were exposed to a pornographic image?

Application Step:

Read Proverbs chapters 5-7 and meditate on the words. Write down anything that stands out as you read. Also, talk to your parents about having a quality filter installed on all the computers in your household. One suggestion is www.bsecure.com

Prayer:

Lord, I want to be a man of purity in my generation. I ask that You help me to see women through Your eyes and not the eyes of our culture. Help me to stand up for Truth even when others see nothing wrong with porn. Please give me the power to overcome any temptation that comes my way... In Jesus' name I pray, amen.

FORGIVENESS
Written by Paul Hart

"But as for you, you meant evil against me; but God meant it for good…"

- Genesis 50:20

Bad Isn't Forever.

You're familiar with the story of Joseph, right? It would be a fair assessment to say that his brothers picked on him a bit… You know, selling him into slavery and all. Sadly, that reminds me a bit of my own childhood. But let's start at the beginning…

My parents were told they could never have children. By the time I came along, the miracle child, they already had 3 adopted sons. That made three big brothers who didn't like the fact that I was their natural born son. Don't get me wrong, unlike the biblical story, my parents didn't show me any special treatment, but it didn't matter to my brothers. They might not have sold me into slavery, but they did pay a taxi cab driver to take me a way (but he brought me back when their money ran out).

Unlike Joseph, I will probably never be in a situation of power over any of my brothers – but God has still used my childhood to make me into the man I am today. I've went through a lot in my life – just like Joseph did, and probably just like you do every day. But God has shown me that family is more important than holding grudges, and forgiveness is the key to happiness.

A lot of bad things happen to us – and if you have brothers, a lot of it probably comes from them. But God uses everything together for the good of those who love Him – even things that others mean to harm us (Rom. 8:28).

Reflection:

Are you focusing solely on the bad things that happen to you, or are you broadening your vision to see the good that come out of it?

Application Step:

Think of something bad that has happened in your past that God has used to help you or someone else later on and remember that the next time something bad happens.

Prayer:

Father God, I get stressed out when things don't go my way. When others are out to get me, or things just seem to be going wrong. Help me to remember that You can use all things for good – even things meant to harm me...

PROVISION

Written by Paul Hart

"For as the heavens are higher than the earth, So are My ways higher than your ways, And My thoughts than your thoughts."
- Isaiah 55:9

So, You Think You Know God?

Let me lighten the mood and tell you a joke.

A man hears about a terrible rain storm coming, and police come by and warn him that he is in the middle of a flood zone. He needs to get his belonging and move to higher ground.

The man says to the police, "It's okay God will provide. I will be just fine."

The rain starts, and the waters rise up past his raised doorstep, and now rescue crews come by pulling boats to put people and their belongings in. They stop and say, "Come on we still have room."

The man just stands there and says, "Its okay, God will provide."

The rain comes down harder now, and everyone has left the area. One guy, who stuck it out as long as he could, gets in his boat and heads out. He finds our man treading water and says, "Get in, I can get you to safety."

But, our man just says, "Its okay God will provide."

Our man dies and goes to the pearly gates to find Jesus waiting for him. Instantly he bee lines it for Jesus saying, "Jesus, I had all my faith in you and God to take care of me, and you just let me die. Why didn't you help me?"

Jesus calmly looks at the man and says, "Did you know the storm was coming? Did the police not try and get you to leave? Did the rescue crews have room for you? And, when everyone else was gone did the one sole person left not come and offer you a ride? WHAT ELSE DID YOU WANT ME TO DO?"

What I am trying to get across to you is that if you truly believe in God, and you truly want Him in your life. You have to be willing to see what He is doing in your life (all around you). He is there to fill your void, to carry you in troubled times, and even when it feels like there is no one left, God is reaching out to you if you just look for Him.

He is not a slap in the face God. He is a patient God, and He will wait for you to listen. Even when you are griping all the time about how He isn't helping you. He may not be telling you what you think you want to hear, but He is there again and again telling you what you need.

Hate to say it, but usually those are two far distant things. When you get it though, and listen fully, it is amazing the feeling of joy that comes into your life from His wisdom.

Reflection:

Is it raining where you're living? Are you in the flood zone? Are you listening to the one who is trying to help you?

Application Step:

Pray and ask God if He's trying to provide for you in a way that you haven't been open to hearing before.

Prayer:

Father God, thank You for always providing for me. Help me to open my eyes to Your provision...

MY FRIEND, WHERE ART THOU

Written by Paul Hart

"In this you greatly rejoice, though now for a little while, if need be, you have been grieved by various trials, that the genuineness of your faith, being much more precious than gold that perishes, though it is tested by fire, may be found to praise, honor, and glory at the revelation of Jesus Christ, whom having not seen you love"
- 1 Peter 1:6-8a

You Never Know What You Have Until You Take It For Granted

Robert was his name. You know that Wingman I talked to you about several devotions ago. He was mine. He was the Hispanic me in every sense of the word. We had each other's backs, but yet we competed for everything. Not to prove better than the other (well maybe a little) but mostly to challenge the other to do better. We even went after the same girl. Even in this area we stopped what we were doing and made a deal. If one of us got to go out with her, the other couldn't be mad. I always thought I would win, but secretly hoped he would because that guy deserved to feel happy.

I won, and to this day I resent the day I won. I had the girl and lost my best friend.

See, Robert was happy for me but he was still bummed. Who wouldn't be, right. I didn't go for the kill and rub it in. She was friends with both of us. I wasn't going to ruin that. No, I did worse. I got the word that she liked me more than a friend and ran with it. I spent all day with my new girl. Let the angels rejoice, someone actually liked me more than just as a friend.

That night, Robert wanted to hang out. I could hear it in his voice. He wasn't feeling too good about himself. I was too psyched up though. She wanted to hang out with me that night, and I wasn't going to let that go. I told him that, too. Not to be mean, but I asked his permission. I told him tomorrow, I was all his. No if ands or buts about it. He understood (or so he said) and I told him bye.

I never got another chance to say anything else to him. He was in a car accident, and worst of all he <u>didn't</u> die. At least not right away. No, he was taken to the hospital, and put on machines. His parents had to watch as his conscious mind drifted away.

My wingman. Myself in another skin. My best friend. A vegetable under hospital covers. I told him I was sorry. I told him he was more important than any girl in the world. I told him a lot, but my actions before said otherwise. I had known this guy since I was 6yrs old, and it was our senior year. We were going to go to college together, and we were going to do miracles in this world. My wingman…

How do you get over something like that?

Why did God do this to someone who didn't deserve it?

Why on Earth did God let him go out with us ending like that?

They're in a better place! To hell with that! I want them in this place!!!

I can't even say to his face I am sorry!!!!

I miss that guy just as much today as the day they pulled the plug. But over the years I've learned the answers to some of the questions I faced back then, and I want to share them with you.

How do you get over something like that? You don't. But, if you really do listen to God and really let love rule your thoughts instead of self-absorbed thoughts. You find ways to learn from what happened, to honor the one you lost, and to remember them for all the great things they did.

Why did God do this to someone who didn't deserve it? It is never what a good person or bad person we are that answers this question. I wanted to know why it wasn't me. I was way worse than him. What kind of friend was I? Then I finally (after quite some time) realized that no matter how long or how short a time we have on Earth, the lasting memories left behind are actually presents to carry with us for as long as we live. Yes, someone is gone, and yes they feel no more pain. If they were alive and you were dead, would you want them to go through what you are putting yourself through? I seriously doubt it. Weather we are given a hundred years to live on Earth or 3 days. God's true gift is that those around you got to live with and through you for that time. When the pain ebbs and your mind is ready to listen and learn. Think of what a pleasure you had with them, and what a gift you were for them as well as they were a gift to you. Enjoy every day God gives with those around you. See the Joy that is out there.

Why on Earth did God let him go out with us ending like that? That's not fair… Not like that… That was a one-time thing… We never did that to each other… Why now… That my friend is guilt talking. That is me feeling sorry for what I did. That is not God's doing. What I got from that is, even in my big mistakes… My friend, Robert, would have forgiven me no matter what if he was alive. Real friends never stay mad at each other. He was really my friend, and I was his. I may not be happy with what I did, but I do everything in my power to not repeat that if I can.

They're in a better place… I was so sick of people telling me that. How do they know? Did they see him in that better place, or were they just talking to be heard? What do they know any way? He wasn't their best friend.

I have to know that Robert was a great guy, a great friend (and not just to me), and an amazing son to his mom and dad. I pray all the time that God is taking real good care of my best friend. Others are feeling it too you know. They don't know what to say any more than you do. So they comfort themselves by comforting you. If you know that the one you're missing this much was so great, don't forget others probably do to. They want to be there for you. Don't drown yourself in sorrow to see that you can be there for them too. Robert would have said the same of me.

I can't even say to his face, "I am sorry." I don't know if I can ever fully forgive myself for putting myself before a friend. I honor him every chance I get, but not out of guilt. I honor him because there are so many in this world who will never have the blessing of know Robert (Bobby) Vasques. I feel like they should know a little bit, just to brighten their lives, if even for a moment. God gave me a gift, and I intend on sharing it with everyone I can. I will always have him in me, just as God intended. It's what I do with his memory that makes it a blessing or a punishment. My choice.

Reflection:

When bad things happen in your life – when you make bad choices – do you choose to dwell on the bad, or can do you allow God to use it for good?

Application Step:

Do you believe the Bible is true? Look up Romans 8:28 and try to see that in your own life – especially when things go wrong or you make mistakes.

Prayer:

Father, I screw up all the time. I make mistakes – sometimes big ones that I regret for a long time. Please remind me that I can choose to live in my mistakes, or I can allow You to take them and use them for Your glory...

IDLE WORDS
Written by Paul Hart

"But I say to you that for every idle word men may speak, they will give account of it in the day of judgment."
- Matthew 12:36

But That's Not What I Meant...

Have you ever had someone use something you said against you? Maybe they repeat something you said, but twist it to mean something different? Or maybe they took something you said as a joke seriously?

Jesus warns in Matthew 12 that our words are important – more important than we may realize. Explaining them to our parents or a teacher, or clearing up a misunderstanding with our friends is just the beginning, we will eventually have to explain them to God as well.

In Ephesians 4 Paul writes: "Let no corrupting talk come out of your mouths, but only such as is good for building up, as fits the occasion, that it may give grace to those who hear." (vs. 29 ESV) Or as my mom would say, "If you can't say anything nice, don't say anything at all." Idol threats and mean jokes clearly don't fit the bill.

But Paul took it even a step farther – he said to only say what is fit for the occasion and gives grace to those around you…

A truly wise man knows when not to speak at all – sometimes we speak to be heard, even though it might be better to say nothing at all. In the words from Proverbs 17:28…

"Even a fool is counted wise when he holds his peace; When he shuts his lips, he is considered perceptive."

I don't know that I've thought of my words that way before, but in order to accomplish it, I'm going to have to start stopping and thinking before I speak.

Reflection:

Do you ever say things you don't mean?

Application Step:

Spend today paying extra attention to what you say. Check to see if it measures up to Ephesians 4:29, and remember that someday you'll stand before Jesus and be reminded of the words you speak today.

Prayer:

Lord, help me to stop and think before I speak. I'm going to need reminded that my words are important and that even joking around can go too far too fast. Help me with my words, God…

POOR ME

Written by Paul Hart

"My dear brothers and sisters, take note of this: Everyone should be quick to listen, slow to speak and slow to become angry, because human anger does not produce the righteousness that God desires."
- James 1:19-20

Don't You Hate Cleaning Up Other Peoples Messes?

I hate when others just don't pull their wait. Just ride on my hard work, and get paid the same as me. That is so unfair. Why do I do more and get paid the same? I don't want to have to clean up after others. I am not their servant.

Oh, but wait, I am asked to be a servant to my fellow man. I am asked to be humble. I am asked to be slow to anger and quick to help. That is so unfair...

Pride is the only thing that makes this not fair. Think of all the things you can do to help the people your with, instead of thinking of all the things they are doing wrong.

Maybe they don't know how to do the job right. You may think something is easy, but to others it may not be. Teach them what you know. By making them better you find that they help more. Usually when others seem to be lazy, it's just the fact that they are embarrassed to ask how to do it because others have not been helpful.

Be the servant, and show them what Jesus taught. To believe in helping others as Jesus would have.

Maybe others are not as slow as you think, but you are trying to steal the show by showing how much better you are. A humble heart has room to allow others to succeed even when it holds us back. In the end of a humble teaching you win twice. You help someone learn a trade as well as you or maybe even better, and you get a new friend who is willing to help you in return when things are tough. How is that a bad thing?

To be slow to anger and quick to help, is probably the number one way to have a winning team. Expect the best of others, and be willing to get them to that point will lead you to a whole new level of joy. When you start thinking how hard it is on you, and how things are just not fair for you, is when Satan has his Apple with your name on it. It is the one thing that will take you from what God wishes. Would you rather live in Eden, cast yourself in to a world of 'poor me's that will do nothing but make you miserable.

Work and life are one in the same. Your actions in the everyday, is just as much a battle a work. In life, the way you handle others and yourself will be the key as if you enjoy what is given you, or you fight tooth and nail to keep yourself unhappy. It's your choice.

Understand that people don't make you miserable. You are the only one who can allow that in your life. People are just like you. Everyone, wants to feel happy. Everyone wants to be able to live in a world where they are not poor, not tired, and definitely not alone.

You can't be poor if you are surrounding yourself and others with God's love. You have to remember a time when everything was going so well it felt like you could burst out of your skin with energy. If you put that effort into people around you so that they can feel that energy, you will feel like you can fly. Never be tired again. Lastly, by putting out that helping hand to others you surround yourself with people who want to do the same in return. God is with you and in you. To teach others of him and show by example his love, you will see his work grow. You will never be alone for God is with you. Imagine if others you know feel the same way.

Will life always come up smelling like roses, and unicorns run free in the fields. Will everything be perfect every day?

Yes… In some fantasy book somewhere it will.

God has not promised to baby us. He has promised us that He will be there to help us. He has also promised us that there will be hardship and persecution. Some people really don't want to hear about God. Some couldn't care less weather you live or die. And, some will be so jealous of your humble nature that they will target you to try and make you feel miserable all over again.

There are those out there that live moment by moment in the poor me stage, that none of the light of God will be heard. That is why the actions that we take play such an important role. You can talk all day of God, but if you actions don't back your words you might as well be talking of Zeus in Greek Mythology for all they will believe you.

It is our struggles that define us, and it is our actions during those struggles that show the real power of our Living Lord. He lives in you, and if you are not strong enough to handle things on your own (which you're not), then show the real strength in you and cast your struggles onto God. Don't ask for help if you don't want it though, for that is just another road to poor me when you don't hear what you want to hear. Ask with a humble heart, and hear where God is leading. Define yourself, encourage others, and bask in the warmth of our One True Lord.

He lives...
So should you...

Reflection:

If work and life are the same battle, how do you want to look at those around you? What is your work ethic like?

Application Step:

If you've been blaming others for your anger, confess that to God and ask Him to give you a humble heart.

Prayer:

Father, please help me to let go of my anger. You teach us to turn the other cheek and go the extra mile. Help me to remember those things when I'm tempted to become angry. Help me to work hard with a humble heart and be slow to anger...

SPIRITUAL DEHYDRATION

Written by CJ Hitz

"On the last and greatest day of the festival, Jesus stood and said in a loud voice, "Let anyone who is thirsty come to me and drink."

- John 7:37

Are you thirsty?

As an avid runner, I've experienced my fair share of dehydration. On one of those occasions, I was doing a training run on a trail in Pinckney, Michigan when I took a wrong turn. Consequently, the wrong turn added 5 miles to what was supposed to be a 13 mile run. My water bottle was empty at around the 12 mile mark which normally would have been fine except for the wrong turn.

I was now starting to experience the classic signs of dehydration…
- Dry mouth
- Lack of urine output (tried to pee but nothing came out)
- Muscles starting to cramp (especially my hamstrings)
- Thirst

Simply being thirsty is a sign we haven't been drinking enough. The body has a way of sounding the alarm in areas that need attention. Needless to say, my body was sounding the alarm long before I made it back to the car! By the time I finished, I had already been doing what I call the "zombie shuffle." In other words, I was like a dead man walking as my body cried out for moisture.

43

When it comes to our relationship with God, sometimes we can find ourselves spiritually dry. There have been many times in my life when I sought to quench my thirst outside of God only to be left with greater thirst. Some classic signs of spiritual dehydration include…

- Irritability
- Lack of patience
- Lack of peace
- Lack of love
- Extreme thirst that can only be quenched by Jesus

Jesus himself calls us to quench our spiritual thirst in Him as the opening verse above says. In the next verse he says,

"Whoever believes in me, as Scripture has said, rivers of living water will flow from within them." (John 7:38)

In other words, when we place our trust in Jesus and walk with him daily, we should never be thirsty for the things of the world. Those outside of Christ are in a constant state of spiritual dehydration as they dig for water in a vast desert.

Even as followers of Jesus, we can sometimes find ourselves looking in the wrong places for water as Jeremiah 2:13 says,

"My people have committed two sins: They have forsaken me, the spring of living water, and have dug their own cisterns, broken cisterns that cannot hold water."

God wants us to find our satisfaction in Him alone. The next time you're tempted to quench your thirst with things like money, porn, a girlfriend, or sports, remember how dry they left you previously.

Reflection:

What are some ways you've tried to quench your thirst only to be left feeling more thirsty and dry?

Application Step:

The next time you're physically thirsty and grab a drink, use it as a reminder to spend a few minutes with Jesus in order to quench your spiritual thirst.

Prayer:

Lord, I'm sorry for running to temporary things in order to satisfy my eternal thirst. I'm tired of feeling spiritually dry. Give me a hunger and thirst for you alone! Help me to be an example for my thirsty friends as they see me drinking in the Living Water. I agree with the Psalmist who proclaimed, *"As the deer pants for streams of water, so my soul pants for you, my God."* (Psalm 42:1)

Expectancy vs. Faith

Written by Paul Hart

"... I declare to you the gospel which I preached to you, which also you received and in which you stand, by which also you are saved, if you hold fast that word which I preached to you—unless you believed in vain."

- 1 Corinthians 15:1-2

How Do You Look At Christ?

It's not how well we did in life – not how much we did for God – but whether or not we trusted in Jesus. That's it. God did it all through Christ, we just have to accept it.

You can't go out and do anything you want and just ask for forgiveness. Your heart and soul must really feel sorry for what you did.

Can you imagine going out and getting drunk, stealing your parent's car and wrapping it around a tree? Then, just walk up to them with a cocky grin on your face and saying, "Sorry folks, I don't know what I was thinking. I'll probably never do that again. Can you get me another car, I really hate walking." What do you think the answer will be?

We treat God like that every day. Pray that He gets me this, or bails me out of that. Our belief in Him is about as expectant as if He was a jolly old fat man with a red suite and white beard. He is not one to be looked on as the bearer of the best presents, but the Savior of souls. The One who bore all our sins.

No one believes in Christ, without letting Christ into them and letting His light shine through them. You can't know what is expected of you without listening to His Word. And, you can't expect to forgiveness without repentance. You have to believe in Him, and in doing that walk in the footsteps of our Lord and Savior.

This is not as easy as it first seemed is it? That is why we talk of strength in such a way. This takes real strength, real love, and real faith. Believe in Him, follow Him, and walk in footsteps that He laid before you. These are not shoes you can easily fill, but that is why forgiveness is His promise to you. You keep trying to do His will, and live in His Words and you will have His everlasting love and forgiveness.

Reflection:

Are you living out the gospel, or are you trying to earn your own way for your own purpose?

Application Step:

Trust God to get you into heaven – just give it all to Him.

Prayer:

Father God, I have been trying so hard to be what You want me to be. I want to live a life worthy of You, but so often I forget the gospel – Your gospel. I forget that You knew I was unworthy, so You sent Your Son to be worthy for me. Thank You for that. Help me to surrender to You and accept the way that You have made for me...

An Example Worth Following

Written by CJ Hitz

"Whoever is kind to the poor lends to the LORD, and he will reward them for what they have done."

- Proverbs 19:17

A Story of Generosity

When I was a kid growing up in the small logging town of Myrtle Creek, Oregon, I had the opportunity to watch several instances of generosity that have stuck with me ever since. They involved my dad and a homeless man named "Claude."

Claude would roam the highways and byways on his worn out bicycle and a huge pack with all of his earthly belongings. I am still amazed at how the man was able to pedal his bike with that load on his back!

On many occasions, while accompanying my dad as he drove into town, we would see Claude riding on the side of the road. Typically, dad would pull ahead and stop alongside the road to wait for Claude. It was about this time that I would shrink into my seat for fear of being noticed by any of my friends.

To be honest, I was embarrassed to be seen with this "hobo" of a guy who had the odor of someone who had not taken a shower in years. My friends and I had nicknames for many of the "colorful characters" wandering our area. Claude was simply known as "Dirt Claude" – as in a clump of dirt.

But my dad saw through the dirt. He saw a man who still deserved to be treated with dignity and respect, regardless of the circumstances that led to his homelessness. As Claude would ride up next to our truck, dad would actually step out and greet him. I can still see Claude's big toothless smile as he would say, "Hey Kenny, good to see you."

They would chat for 15-20 minutes before dad would almost always put a $20 bill in Claude's hand and give him a hug upon saying goodbye. Neither of them ever seemed in a rush. Claude would soak up the attention that every human being craves and my dad was more than willing to offer. It was generosity that went beyond just money.

One day my dad came home with some sad news. "Claude died yesterday." My heart sank as I thought about how often people made fun of Claude, myself included. "Apparently, they found Claude frozen to death under an overpass...said his body was as hard as an ice cube."

As hard as an ice cube.

Those words still ring in my ears to this day. What a lonely, agonizing way to spend your last hours on this earth. Claude could not have been older than 30. It very well could be that my dad was the last kind face Claude ever saw before his passing.

After all these years, my dad's actions remain a powerful and vivid example of rich generosity not easily found in our world. It's the kind of generosity that Jesus demonstrated daily during the 33 years he walked on this earth.

It's an example worth following.

Reflection:

Do you have any examples of people in your life who have shown loving generosity? What has been the greatest act of generosity you've ever witnessed?

Application Step:

Who are the people in your school, neighborhood or town who remind you of Claude? In other words, the people who get picked on, ignored or bullied? Think of ways you could bless their lives and make them feel like they matter. Perhaps you have another brother or sister in Christ that could help you brainstorm ideas.

Prayer:

Lord, thank you for giving us the ultimate example of generosity by laying down your life in order that we might have eternal life. I'm sorry for all the times I've ignored those in need or even been part of making fun of them. I ask that you give me your eyes of compassion as I look at the world around me. May my life be a blessing to others. In Jesus' name I pray, Amen.

CONTENTMENT
Written by Paul Hart

"Not that I speak from want, for I have learned to be content in whatever circumstances I am."

- Philippians 4:11

Happiness Isn't About The Next Best Thing.

I have had the worst problems in my past with impatience for something better. Whether it was getting a better position at work, or a nicer T.V., etc. etc... I could never understand why everyone had these nice things while I just got by. It was so so so not fair!!!

Wanting the better life and to feel like I was going somewhere in the world just seemed to me to be the way it should be. I couldn't see how people who lied and stepped all over others always seemed to have a leg up on me. Why the kids born into money always seemed to have the easy life, and I had to be happy with hand me downs and garage sale bests.

I had a chance finally to go all out my freshman year of college. I (not by choice) had saved up almost $10,000 for college by the time I graduated high school. Let me explain that this was accomplished by my parents taking every paycheck I ever made in high school and putting it away in an account I couldn't touch. I also had some amazing friends of the family and relatives who gave me money for graduation. My parents (very begrudgingly) let me have it after graduation and away I went to college. Wooo Whooo!!!

A kid who, in his mind, had had nothing his whole life, now felt as rich as an Arab Sheik, and went on a spending spree and a drinking binge. I literally spent the entire $10,000 in one semester. No wooo whoo... But, I had the newest line of jeans, shirts and what not that 1990 had to offer. I might have been broke, but I was going to look good on the way down poverty lane.

Then God gave me a wakeup call that I didn't want to wake up to right away. I, being the college freshman type, waited tell I had no clothes clean before I did laundry, took everything I owned to the laundry in the dorm laundromat. While waiting for all the washing machines to finish I got hungry. I had a few minutes till they were done and went to grab a bite to eat. Snacked on a quick burger, and booked it back to get my clothes.

Hey look, someone opened every washing machine in the room. Hey look, something seems to be missing. Hey look, apparently they were not impressed enough with my stylish undies and socks to take those too. How nice of them to leave them for me.

In my grief, I turned a tearful eye to heaven and said, "My world is over. I have spent my money and now have nothing to show for it. My image is ruined..."

Did I learn anything right then and there? No, short of just feeling sorry for myself. I didn't get what was being said. Now, looking back, I see that I really didn't miss any of those things. I got on with life, and figured out how to get by with hand me downs (this time from friends) and garage sale bests.

I was never so happy in my life to have the shirt on my back and good friends. Life really wasn't all that bad even though I, supposedly, lost everything. I look in disappointment at the fact I wasted all that money on things that once gone, meant nothing at all to me.

I have learned that all the efforts my parents were putting into me, were falling on deaf ears and a weak self-image. All I wanted was the next best thing, and I was going to have it at any cost. The next best things have come and gone throughout my life, and honestly I don't miss a single one. I am amazed to feel God's presence in my life after all the incredibly selfish and insane things I have done, but yet there He is.

I have a family and friends, and get to spend as much time with my aging parents as I can to let them know I grew up some at 42, and I now appreciate so much of what they tried to teach me. Not everything mind you. I haven't grown up all the way. Just ask my wife. She'll tell you.

Your gifts are all around you, and the day will come where you will start to see past the "poor me". Open your heart and see for a second if you will really miss the things you really want, or if God is leading you to the wonderful things you can't live without.

Reflection:

Are the things you want more important than the things you need? Are you wise enough to know the difference?

Application Step:

Think about what true happiness really is. Write down a list of things that make you happy in your life right now that you are thankful for.

Prayer:

Father, help me to be content where I am. Show me the difference between wants and needs – and help me to put value in the things that truly matter...

THE 7 CHURCHES

Written by Paul Hart

"No one can serve two masters; for either he will hate the one and love the other, or else he will be loyal to the one and despise the other..."

- Matthew 6:24

Which One Are You?

Tucked away at the end of the Bible is the book of Revelation. In the first few chapters, it talks about 7 churches. The churches of Ephesus, Smyrna, Pergamum, Thyatira, Sardis, Philadelphia, and Laodicea. Each of these 7 churches had a problem that Jesus wanted to address.

Ephesus – The Loveless Church. Jesus chastised this church for "leaving their first love." This church use to be on fire for Jesus – and now... not so much.

So many of us start off on fire for Christ, but let it dwindle with time. If you've lost your love for Christ, the message Jesus had for this church, may be for you too.

Smyrna – The Suffering Church. This church was being persecuted, they were poor, and nothing was going their way. Jesus' message to them was just to hold fast to Him. To keep the faith even when the going was tough.

How many of us can relate to that? Life isn't always easy – we struggle with a ton of things. Kids at school may mock us for being Christians or because our parents can't afford the nicest shoes. If you're struggling in this area – the message Jesus wrote to this church, might just be for you too.

Pergamum – The Compromising Church. These Christians lived in a city that worshiped Greek gods – I mean REALLY worshiped them. If you weren't serving a Greek god, you were in trouble – so they compromised. And Jesus said that was not the cool thing to do by Him. He wanted them to stand firm in their faith and stand up for what they believed in.

Is that a message that you need to hear? Have you been caving when it comes to your beliefs? Maybe you saw a movie you knew you shouldn't, or spoke words you knew didn't honor God. If you're having trouble standing up for your faith, you might need to hear the words Jesus spoke to the church of Pergamum.

Thyatira – The Tolerant Church. We live in a world that teaches tolerance, so this is something that's hard to hear. Jesus got onto this church for tolerating false teachers and immorality. With the world today, this message is one we all need. Do the preachers you listen to teach the Truth – or do they pollute it?

Sardis – The Dead Church. How would you like Jesus to refer to you as dead to Him? If you're a Christian, that's a HUGE problem. Have you ever forgotten that you are a servant of Christ? Becoming a Christian isn't a onetime thing – it's a lifetime commitment.

Philadelphia – The Faithful Church. Finally, a church that Christ is proud of. They still have some problems, they live in an imperfect city, but Jesus says they are doing a good job of living for Him – but He also warns them that it's going to get worse.

Sometimes, when life is good, we get lazy. Then when problems do arise, we aren't ready for them. The warning Jesus gave this church is one that I needed to hear. During the easy times we should be training for what's to come – not going on vacation.

Laodicea – The Lukewarm Church. Jesus tells this church that He would rather they were either on fire for Him, or completely cold – He doesn't want us to be sitting on the line and kind of Christians. He either wants us all, or nothing at all to quote a country song.

Reflection:

Which church are you most similar to and what do you need to do about it?

Application Step:

Read through Revelation chapters 2 and 3 where Jesus is addressing the churches. And find out if there is something He is warning you about through those letters.

Prayer:

Dear Jesus, help me to be on fire for You. Help me to stand strong in my faith and live a life that brings You glory…

CHRISTIAN WORKS

Written by Paul Hart

*"For we are His workmanship, created in Christ Jesus
for good works, which God prepared beforehand that we should
walk in them."*

\- Ephesians 2:10

Are your expectations higher than Gods?

Our youth pastor recently asked us a question. It was a fill in the blank sort of thing. So I want to ask you to fill in the blank too.

You can't be a Christian if _____ .

Did you put anything in that blank? Maybe it's if you have tattoos, or drinks alcohol. Maybe it's because you cut or smoke. Maybe you've gone too far with a girl (or 10).

Now let me tell you what he said next – because it's important.

Being a Christian is not about you – it's about Christ.

The Bible says that Jesus did it all on the cross. Yes, it's good to live by God's rules and to dedicate our lives to Him. God wants us to honor Him – but even when we fail, Jesus already accomplished our salvation. He did it all. It's finished.

Now you might be thinking, "Yeah, but..." There are no buts. Either Jesus did it all or He didn't. It's not your morals, church attendance, or good behavior – those are fruits of the gospel, not a way to salvation.

God's Word says that we were saved for good works, not by good works. Being a Christian isn't about anything other than Christ. Not for you, and not for anyone else.

Reflection:

Are your qualifications for being a Christian different than Gods?

Application Step:

If you have any sin that you have been letting stand between you and God, confess it to Him and acknowledge that it no longer stands between you and your Salvation.

Prayer:

Father God, thank you for sending Your Son to die for my sins. I get hung up on myself and think I know what You require better than You do. Help me to remember that nothing can stand in between us – and thank You for being so forgiving...

INTELLIGENCE

Written by Paul Hart

"For all that is in the world—the lust of the flesh, the lust of the eyes, and the pride of life—is not of the Father but is of the world."
- 1 John 2:16

Earthly Intelligence vs. Godly Intelligence

We go through our days trying to find ways to fix our problems. We love to find ways to blame our Parents for our problems. We have this terrible habit of turning to the world of psychologists and counselors to get answers to problems we often created for ourselves - all by ourselves. It is the way we were taught as children. Mom and Dad always knew how to fix our messes and in the case of my kids fix everything they break. People always seem to have all the answers when we are small. Why shouldn't it be that way now that we are bigger?

Often I find that other people's answers are inserted into our problems have our lives. A one standard fits all kind of thing. It makes those who gave us the answer feel more important and justified for what they do. Throughout the Bible, for hundreds and thousands of years, people have taken the words of God and written them down. Yet nowhere in that book will you find anything that tells us that drugs will fix all evils, or that we can do it all all on our own.

We want the quick fix, vs. the true fix. Who needs the Holy Spirit, right? Our belief in self is far easier to imagine, than a belief that someone could love us enough to give up His life for us. We believe that outward beauty is soooo much more important than a true belief that we are more in the Spirit of Christ.

Morals are outdated, and modesty is a thing of the past. Didn't you hear on the commercial... "We are facing a real problem today. Women are getting hotter!" Is that really the truth or is it that the standards for what women wear has fallen to an all-time low?

We can't have God in school, but yet they still want us to practice all the morals behind what God teaches. We can't have God in the pledge, but we want everyone to love thy fellow man - also taught by God.

The way man thinks is still so child-like, we should really turn to the Father with the experience. His words are in writing, and with true humble thinking. If we want to know the answers to our everyday lives, the Good Book is a practiced and true way of looking at life.

We have looked to our parents to guide us when we were small. It is time to draw on the experience of our Father to guide us now.

Reflection:

Do you really think you know more than what has been laid before you in the Bible, or is it just easier to think this way than to do what you know is right through what it says?

Application Step:

The next time you're faced with a problem, stop to find out what the Bible has to say on the subject. You can ask your pastor or youth leader if you need help.

Prayer:

Father, give me the wisdom find help in Your Word and not in the words of the world...

GIRLS VS. CARS

Written by Paul Hart

"Let us behave properly as in the day, not in carousing and drunkenness, not in sexual promiscuity and sensuality, not in strife and jealousy."

- Romans 13:13 NASB

That's A No Go On The Test Drive.

I knew a pastor who use to say that girls are not like sports cars. We shouldn't be going after the hottest model, taking test drives, or checking out under the hood. God didn't make them with the idea that we would trade them in every few years.

It's true that the Bible says that God created women for men – He designed our relationship. Yet He designed us to choose one woman to love and cherish forever. I'm not saying that dating is wrong. Far from it. It can be a prelude to a deeper relationship. But, (to coin a joke) girls are not doorknobs, everyone doesn't need a turn. Dating should be more of strengthening a friendship and not about hooking up. I know that goes completely against our modern culture – but that's God's plan. It always has been and always will be.

The Bible says that Jesus is the same yesterday, today and forever (Heb. 13:8). He doesn't change His standards based off of what's popular – in fact, He was crucified for going against the flow and standing up for God's standards – standards that are also the same yesterday, today and forever.

In Genesis, the Bible says that God created women because it wasn't good for men to be alone. He created them as our equals. He created one woman for one man. And He created them to love one another. Girls are trying to figure out what they are looking for just as much as we are. And they deserve the same respect we want for ourselves.

So now it's up to us. Will we choose to go with the flow and treat chicks like cars – or will we stand up for God's plan and start treating them with respect?

Reflection:

Do you look at girls the same way you look at cars, or do you value them for who they really are?

Application Step:

Spend time praying for the girls you're closest with. If they don't know Christ, pray for them to find Him. If they do know Him, pray that they grow stronger in Him. And no matter what, pray that you see them for who they really are.

Prayer:

Father God, thank You for creating girls. Help me to look at them as Your creation – Your daughters. Remind me that they were designed to be loved, not used, when I forget. And help me to see them for who they really are… In Jesus' name I pray, amen.

BATTLEGROUND

Written by Paul Hart

"Put on the full armor of God, so that you will be able to stand firm against the schemes of the devil. For our struggle is not against flesh and blood, but against the rulers, against the powers, against the world forces of this darkness, against the spiritual forces of wickedness in the heavenly places."
- Ephesians 6:11-12 NASB

The Cliff Notes...

Man, it's a jungle out there. It feels like you're fighting parents, teachers, hormones, trusting people, and setting yourself apart from all of this to be noticed. There just isn't enough time in the day to take on all this by yourself. What are you going to do?

I have to tell you from personal experience that taking the Rocky Balboa stance just leads to 5 broken hands, a broken nose, a broken cheek bone, separated ribs, and a whole list of other things I don't want to bore you with. In the end I look back and think, "Dear God!! What was I fighting so hard against?" It also gives me all kinds of ammo to use with my kids to remind them that from all mistakes, wisdom can come. Please, learn from mine without copying the truly hard parts. Call this the Cliff Notes...

I have learned one valuable thing above all others from my temporary insanity days. Pride can tear down all things that God wants for you.

- Parents Just Don't Understand... is just another way of saying I want it my way, not yours!

- Teachers Have No Clue What Their Talking About... is just another way to say I am bored with sitting in this room when I could be out hanging with my friends!

- Hormones... I'm more man than you are, let me prove it to you any way I have to!

- People Always Let Me Down... is just another way of saying I don't want to take a chance of looking bad. I have an image to uphold!

- Be An Individual, Not Just One Of The Crowd... is just another way of saying I have no clue what others are thinking, so I'll give up on even trying and make myself look like a man!

Now comes the hard part. Is your pride going to rule you or are you going to let God in and learn to be the humble soul you're asked to be. Ouch!!! People just walk all over the weak people in this world. It's a dog eat dog, and I don't want to be the tuck tail wimp at school.

Look at the example set for you by Jesus. Turn the other cheek, make yourself a servant, and the humble shall rule the heavens.

Was this guy a wimp, or was he the King of Kings?

Your true strength comes from your faith in God, and your belief in what He asks of you that carries you through. Not your image. Here is a quick example of how weak your image is.

Picture this:

> Here is the Captain of the Football Team and Home Coming King. All the kids at school look up to him, and all the girls want him. After he graduates High School he is terrified to leave small town USA and strike out in the big world.
>
> Why?
>
> Here he is someone, and everyone knows him. There, he is a no one, and he has to start over. Why would he want to do that?
>
> How important is image now?

Your belief, and strength will be tested every day, and will go with you no matter where you go. Your pride and image are passing, and that's luggage you can't take with you everywhere.

Reflection:

Is it really that important to build on something so easy to tear down?

Application Step:

The next time you're feeling frustrated or exasperated, stop and think about whether it's your pride speaking or if you're responding in humbleness.

Prayer:

Father God, help me to have the heart of a servant and to care more about helping those around me than helping myself…

TRUE STRENGTH

Written by Paul Hart

"Be of good courage, And He shall strengthen your heart, All you who hope in the Lord."

- Psalm 31:24

Strength From Above...

How strong are you – emotionally? Most of the time when we talk about their strength, we're thinking physical. We're taking muscles. But there is more than one type of strength – and emotional strength (also known as the strength of heart) is something that's expected, but easier to bluff than to actually have.

It's the strength it takes to not just stand your ground when the other guys start making fun of you but to not let it affect you.

It's the strength it takes to stand up for what you believe in, without cowering on the inside.

But there are two kinds of emotional strength. There's the kind that comes from trusting an awesome God, and the kind that comes from being hardened by the world. And frankly, being hardened by the world isn't really strength at all – it's just a lack of caring. A weakness.

True strength of heart isn't something we can achieve on our own. There isn't some magic weight lifting kit for your heart – in fact, it's much easier to tear your heart up then it is to build it up. And while it's hard to admit that we need help from anyone – especially when we are talking about strength – that's exactly what we have to do. Which is why it takes strength to actually let go of that pride and acknowledge you need Christ in your life. Not just as a way to heaven, but as a way to live a life of strength.

Reflection:

Are you relying on yourself to get you through life, or are you trusting in the strength given to you by your Creator?

Application Step:

If you have never taken the step of surrendering your pride and asking God to give you His strength, do so now. If you're making that decision for the first time, be sure to tell someone – your parents, youth pastor, a friend – anyone.

If you have already done so, take a moment to thank God for giving you the strength to live your life for Him.

Prayer:

Father God, Help me to surrender my pride. Help me to realize that true strength comes from a faith in You – not my own pigheadedness... Give me Your strength today I ask in the name of Your Son. Amen.

CONCLUSION

I have written to you, young men, because you are strong, and the word of God abides in you, and you have overcome the wicked one."

— 1 John 2:14

True strength is about more than how much you can lift – it's about faith in the one true God and His Son, Jesus Christ. We serve an awesome God. He was willing to make the ultimate sacrifice for you and me.

As you move forward in your walk with Christ, we pray that you continue to grow stronger in your faith and walk on a path that leads you closer to Jesus every day.

In closing, we want to leave you with a blessing found in Psalm 91 (vs 14 – paraphrased):

May the words of your mouth and the meditations of your heart always be acceptable in the sight of the Lord, your Strength and Redeemer.

Get more FREE Devotionals For Guys At:
www.FindYourTrueStrength.com/devos

Recommended Resources

Devotions:

Teen Devotionals... for Guys! –
www.FindYourTrueStrength.com/devos

Fuel for the Soul: 21 devotionals that nourish by CJ Hitz

PrayFit by Jimmy Pena

Streams in the Desert by L.B. Cowman

Twenty-One: Video Devotions from Groundwire

Bible Reading Plans:

YouVersion

BibleGateway

WHO'S BEHIND THE BOOK?

Paul & Heather Hart

Paul Hart is just your average pastor's kid. He grew up in church and fought the Lord every step of the way. Fast forward to today and things have changed. Paul and his wife, Heather, serve the Lord side-by-side. Besides writing devotionals and founding the ministry FindYourTrueStrength.com, they also help other Christian authors with designing, publishing and marketing their books.

You can learn more about their ministry at:
www.AuthorsHart.com

CJ & Shelley Hitz

C.J. and Shelley Hitz enjoy sharing God's Truth through their speaking engagements and their writing. On downtime, they enjoy spending time outdoors running, hiking and exploring God's beautiful creation.

To find out more about their ministry or to invite them to your next event, check out their website at:
www.ChristianSpeakers.tv

Share Your Thoughts

We want your feedback!
To let us know what you think
or read what others had to say, visit:
www.FindYourTrueStrength.com

Contact Information:

We would love to hear from you! Send us an e-mail or a letter to the following address:

support@FindYourTrueStrength.com

Paul Hart
P.O. Box 1277
Seymour, TX 76380

Websites:

www.FindYourTrueStrength.com
www.AuthorsHart.com
www.CJHitz.com

21 Teen Devotionals...
For Girls?

Got a sister?
A female cousin?
A girlfriend or a friend that's a girl?

Paul and CJ's wives, Heather and Shelley,
have written a devotional book for teen girls:

Available on Amazon

Get FREE Devotionals For Guys Via E-mail At:
www.FindYourTrueStrength.com/devos